GLOBAL**HOT**SPOTS

THE
INDIAN
SUBCONTINENT

Paul Mason

MACMILLAN
LIBRARY

First published in 2008 by
MACMILLAN EDUCATION AUSTRALIA PTY LTD
15–19 Claremont Street, South Yarra 3141

Visit our website at www.macmillan.com.au or go directly to www.macmillanlibrary.com.au

Associated companies and representatives throughout the world.

National Library of Australia
Cataloguing-in-Publication data

Mason, Paul, 1967-
The Indian Subcontinent / author, Paul Mason.
South Yarra, Vic. : Macmillan Education, 2008.
ISBN: 978 1 4202 6479 1 (hbk.)
Global hot spots
Includes index.
For primary school age.
Subjects: Culture conflict.
             Political violence.
             Ethnic conflict.
             War.
             War--Religious aspects.
             South Asia--History.
             South Asia--Politics and government.
954

 Produced for Macmillan Education Australia by
MONKEY PUZZLE MEDIA LTD
The Rectory, Eyke, Woodbridge, Suffolk IP12 2QW, UK

Edited by Daniel Rogers
Text and cover design by Tom Morris and James Winrow
Page layout by Tom Morris
Photo research by Lynda Lines
Maps by Martin Darlison, Encompass Graphics
Flags by MPM Images

Printed in China

Acknowledgements
The author and the publisher are grateful to the following for permission to reproduce copyright material:

Front cover photograph: Pakistani protesters shout slogans at a demonstration against President Pervez Musharraf of
Pakistan, July 2007. Courtesy of Getty Images (Arif Ali).

Corbis, pp. **4** (Amit Gupta/Reuters), **8** (Bob Krist), **10** (Bettmann), **12** (Stapleton Collection), **16** (Bettman), **18** (Bettman), **23**
(Zahid Hussein/Reuters), **24** (Andrees Latif/Reuters), **26** (Dexter Cruez), **27** (Anuruddha Lokuhapuarachchi/Reuters), **28**
(Abir Abdullah/epa), **29** (Inter Services Public Relations/Handout/epa); Corbis Digital Stock, p. **9**; Getty Images, pp. **7** (AFP),
11 (Hulton Archive), **14** (Hulton Archive), **15** (Hulton Archive), **17** (Time & Life Pictures), **19** (Time & Life Pictures), **20** (Hulton
Archive), **21** (AFP), **22** (AFP), **25**; iStockphoto, p. **6**.

While every care has been taken to trace and acknowledge copyright, the publisher tenders their apologies for any
accidental infringement where copyright has proved untraceable. Where the attempt has been unsuccessful, the publisher
welcomes information that would redress the situation.

CONTENTS

Glossary words

When a word is printed in **bold**, you can look
up its meaning in the Glossary on page 31.

ALWAYS IN THE NEWS

Global hot spots are places that are always in the news. They are places where there has been conflict between different groups of people for years. Sometimes the conflicts have lasted for hundreds of years.

Why do hot spots happen?

There are four main reasons why hot spots happen:

1 Disputes over land, and who has the right to live on it.

2 Disagreements over religion and **culture**, where different peoples find it impossible to live happily side-by-side.

3 Arguments over how the government should be organised.

4 Conflict over resources, such as oil, gold or diamonds.

Sometimes these disagreements spill over into violence – and into the headlines.

HOT SPOT BRIEFING

THE INDIAN SUBCONTINENT
The Indian subcontinent is a giant triangle of land that contains India, the largest country, Pakistan, Nepal, Bhutan, Bangladesh and Sri Lanka.

Troops on the border between Indian and Pakistani Kashmir. The territory of Kashmir has been a source of conflict between India and Pakistan since 1947.

The Indian subcontinent

The Indian subcontinent has been a hot spot since 1947. That was when its two biggest countries, India and Pakistan, were formed. The two countries immediately began a conflict over religion and land, which has continued ever since.

One cause of conflict for India and Pakistan is Kashmir. Kashmir is a northern border region that both claim to own. The subcontinent has other conflict zones too, including Bangladesh, Nepal and Sri Lanka.

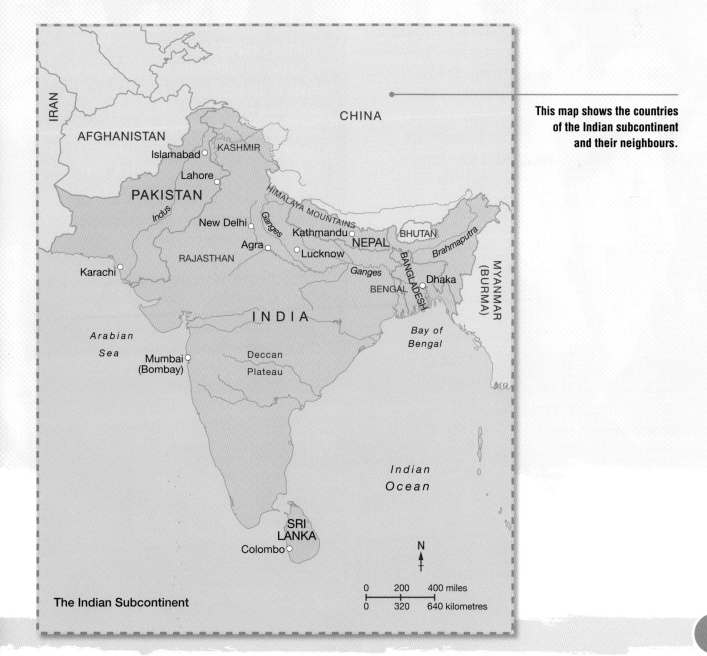

This map shows the countries of the Indian subcontinent and their neighbours.

The Indian Subcontinent

| 0 | 200 | 400 miles |
| 0 | 320 | 640 kilometres |

THE INDIAN SUBCONTINENT

Why is the Indian subcontinent such a hot spot for conflict? One reason is that the region's extremes of religion and wealth divide its people and make it hard for them to live together peacefully.

Language and culture

Many of the subcontinent's peoples speak different languages and have different cultures. This makes it harder for them to communicate, and more likely that arguments will spring up because they do not understand each other. Divisions between the different peoples have sometimes turned into bitter conflicts.

HOT SPOT BRIEFING

A VARIED LANDSCAPE
The Indian subcontinent contains a huge variety of different landscapes.
- Himalaya mountains: the world's highest mountain range
- Northern plains: the fertile plains of great rivers are used for farming. The Thar Desert lies in the west
- Deccan Plateau: low hills and mountains are mainly farmland, with rainforest in the west
- Great cities: the subcontinent's cities are among the fastest growing in the world. They are home to industries of all kinds.

One of the many different landscapes of the Indian subcontinent, with red chilli peppers drying in the sunshine of Rajasthan, India. The subcontinent's landscapes are home to a range of different cultures and religions.

Religions

There is a wide range of religions in the Indian subcontinent. The two biggest religions are Islam and Hinduism. There are also Buddhists, Sikhs, Christians and followers of many other religions. Even when people follow the same religion, they sometimes follow different versions of it. This means that they have often found it difficult to live side-by-side peacefully. Arguments between the religions have led to tens of thousands of deaths over the years.

Rich and poor

One of the biggest divisions throughout the countries of the subcontinent is between rich and poor. Most of the people are very poor but they are often ruled by a small group of people who are extremely rich and powerful. The poor find it hard to improve their chances of earning more or getting a better education, and this situation causes conflicts and sometimes violence.

'"India" is a geographical term. It is no more a united nation than the Equator.'

British Prime Minister Winston Churchill (1874–1965), who felt that the differences between India's people made it impossible for them to act together.

A city scene from Karachi, Pakistan. In both Pakistan and India there are huge cities that are home to millions of people.

AN ANCIENT LAND

The modern countries of the Indian subcontinent were nearly all formed after World War II. However, the land that they occupy is ancient. It was once ruled by some of the world's oldest civilisations.

The Vedic Civilisation

Aryan invaders, who arrived in the north in about 1500 BCE, **founded** the Vedic Civilisation. The Vedic Civilisation is named after the 'Vedic texts'. These are famous writings on which the Hindu religion is based.

The Mughals

From 1526 onwards, the **Mughal Empire** began to take control of the Indian subcontinent. At its height, the empire controlled most of what is now north and central India, Afghanistan, Bangladesh and Pakistan. Today the empire is best known around the world for its **architecture**, including the famous Taj Mahal building.

A Hindu wedding ceremony. The Hindu religion has roots over 3000 years old.

Religion under the Mughals

The Mughals were Muslims, but their **subjects** were mainly Hindu. Many Hindus disliked being ruled by Muslims. Akbar, the second emperor, abolished taxes on Hindus, and employed Hindu generals and officials. This made the Hindus feel happier about being ruled by a Muslim.

The Empire declines

The fifth Mughal emperor, Aurangzeb (1618–1707), thought that everyone should be Muslim. He reintroduced taxes on Hindus and destroyed many Hindu temples. As a result, Hindu warriors began to rebel. The Mughal Empire soon began to fall apart.

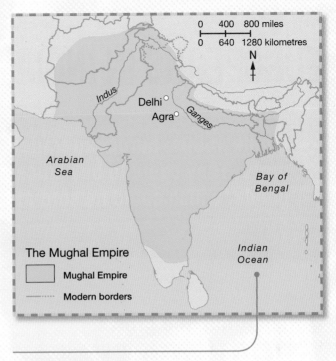

The Mughal Empire

☐ Mughal Empire

------- Modern borders

This map shows the extent of the Mughal Empire at its largest in about 1700.

The Taj Mahal, built in 1653 by the fourth Mughal emperor, Shah Jahan, as a tomb for his beloved wife.

EUROPEANS IN INDIA

By the 1500s, European traders had begun to visit Mughal ports. They came to buy spices, silks and other valuable goods, which could be sold at huge profits in Europe.

British influence grows

By the 1700s, European traders had become very powerful in India. Most powerful of all was the British East India Company. The Company made agreements with the rulers of Indian states that only it would be allowed to trade in their territory.

Decline of the Mughals

During the 1700s, the Mughal Empire began to break up. In many places, the East India Company replaced the Empire as the governing power. By 1774 the Company had become so powerful that one of its men, Warren Hastings, was appointed the first Governor-General of India.

HOT SPOT BRIEFING

THE COMPANY'S ARMED FORCES
The British East India Company's power was backed up by a powerful army and navy. These protected its trade throughout India.

The Battle of Plassey in 1757, where General Clive (with the telescope) of the British East India Company defeated the ruler of Bengal. Many people think that the battle marked the start of British control of India.

The British East India Company in India

The British East India Company wanted to make as much money as possible. This made things difficult for the Indian people. It meant:

- new **taxes** and other changes caused poor farmers to lose their land, and large numbers of Indians to go hungry

- many Indians disliked British officials, who thought that Indians were inferior to them

- some Indian industries were ruined. One example was the clothing industry. The British East India Company bought raw cotton in India, to be made into cloth in England. Many Indian cloth-makers went out of business as a result.

'... an opulent city lay at my mercy... I walked through vaults which were thrown open to me alone, piled on either hand with gold and jewels!'

General Clive of the British East India Company, after the Battle of Plassey in Bengal (now mainly part of Bangladesh) in 1757.

British people outside their house in India. The British tried to create little areas of England wherever they went in India.

THE BRITISH EMPIRE

The British East India Company was unpopular with many Indians. In 1857, this unpopularity flared up into a rebellion that would have long-lasting consequences for the Indian subcontinent.

The Indian rebellion

The Indian rebellion began when some of the Company's Indian troops were given new cartridges to use in their rifles by the British. The soldiers thought the cartridges had been wrapped using cow and pig fat.

Hindus cannot eat cows, and Muslims cannot eat pork. When British officers tried to make the troops use the cartridges, they revolted. The revolt quickly spread across northern and central India, and led to thousands of deaths.

Damage caused by an explosion in Lucknow, India, during the Indian rebellion.

The British Government takes control

In 1858, once the **rebels** had been crushed, the British government decided to take control of India away from the East Indian Company. It took over the Company's territories, and allowed local princes to keep their lands so long as they agreed to British overall rule.

The British eventually controlled an area covering almost the whole Indian subcontinent, including modern-day Pakistan, India, Bangladesh and Sri Lanka. British rule continued until after the end of World War II in 1945.

'The order went out to shoot... The women were all spared but their screams, on seeing their husbands and sons butchered, were most painful.'

Edward Vibart, an officer for the British East India Company, describes fighting against the Indian rebellion.

HOT SPOT BRIEFING

THE RAJ
The British government organisation in India was often called 'The Raj'. Raj means 'rule' or 'administration'.

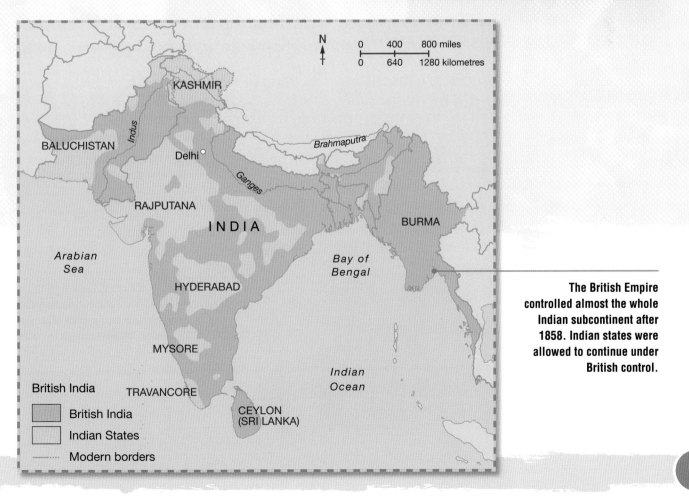

The British Empire controlled almost the whole Indian subcontinent after 1858. Indian states were allowed to continue under British control.

INDEPENDENCE

By the early 1900s, many Indians were demanding that Britain give up control and let them govern themselves. Many different groups were united in this desire for **independence**.

Mahatma Gandhi

Mahatma Gandhi was one of the leaders of the independence movement. Gandhi was a Hindu, and he believed in the Hindu idea of *ahimsa*, which means non-violence. To protest without violence, his followers refused to work for the British, to buy British goods or wear British cloth. Hundreds of thousands of them took part in large marches. As a result of these protests, Gandhi was often arrested by the British.

'Today there begins … a war against the British Raj. What is our name? Mutiny. What is its work? Mutiny. Where will mutiny break out? In India. The time will soon come when rifles and blood will take the place of pen and ink.'

A message from the Ghadar Party, an organisation of Indians living in North America in 1913.

Mahatma Gandhi (with his head bowed) with some of his supporters on a march to protest against the government in 1930.

The Muslim League

The Muslim League also campaigned for independence. There were fewer Muslims than Hindus in India. The League feared that when India became independent, Muslims would be outnumbered by Hindus and have no power. The League wanted India to be split into two countries, one Hindu and one Muslim.

Independence in 1947

After World War II, the British knew that they could no longer hang on to India. Too many Indians opposed British rule, and Britain itself had been weakened by years of war. In August 1947, the British finally gave up control and left.

Indians celebrating the independence of their country in August 1947.

PAKISTAN AND INDIA

When the British left in 1947, India was divided into two countries. The largest part became India, where most Hindus lived. The rest became the mainly Muslim country of Pakistan.

Partition

The division of British India into India and Pakistan is known as **Partition**. Although India was mainly Hindu and Pakistan was mainly Muslim, there were Muslims living in India and Hindus in Pakistan. After Partition, the rivalry and dislike between Hindus and Muslims flared up into violence.

Desperate to escape the violence, people crowded onto trains that would take them to areas that were safe for their religion. However, many people were killed at train stations while they waited to travel to safety.

After Partition, millions of Hindus, Muslims and Sikhs moved from India to Pakistan or Pakistan to India. Many travelled by train. If there was no room inside they even crowded on to the roof.

Violence in border areas

When India and Pakistan became independent, the exact borders between them had not been agreed. As a result, violence flared up in many border areas. In mainly Muslim areas, people tried to force Hindus and Sikhs to leave. In mainly Hindu areas it was the Muslims who were forced out.

A long line of bullock carts carrying Hindu refugees from Pakistan to India.

THE MOVEMENT OF MILLIONS

Millions of people moved across the borders between India and Pakistan in the months following Partition.

From India to Pakistan
7 226 000 Muslims

From Pakistan to India
7 249 000 Hindus and Sikhs

WAR IN KASHMIR

Nowhere was the conflict between Pakistan and India more bitter than in Kashmir. Kashmir is a continuing source of argument between the two countries because they disagree about who should govern it.

Kashmir in 1947

When the British left India in 1947, Kashmir's Hindu ruler did not decide whether his territory should become part of India or Pakistan. Kashmir is a continuing source of argument between the two countries because they cannot agree on who should govern it. Fearing that he was about to lose power, Kashmir's ruler decided to become part of India. Pakistani and Indian forces joined the fighting, and two years of war between the two countries followed, as the two countries battled for control of Kashmir.

Ceasefire

The two sides declared a **ceasefire** on 1 January 1949. The **United Nations** (UN) decided on a dividing line between Indian-held Kashmir and Pakistani-held Kashmir. Even so, both sides continued to claim that Kashmir belonged to them.

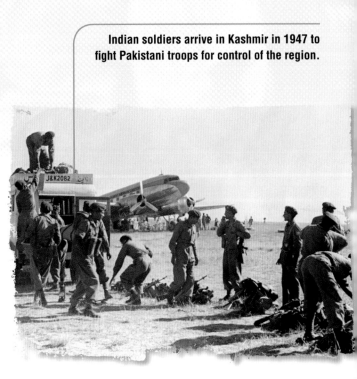

Indian soldiers arrive in Kashmir in 1947 to fight Pakistani troops for control of the region.

'Whether they are under India, Pakistan or independent ... for Kashmiris it's more important to have peace.'

A contributor to a worldaffairsboard Internet discussion on Kashmir (16 November 2004).

Kashmir today

Today, Kashmir is a battleground. Indian and Pakistani troops face each other across the dividing line, and they often fire shots at one another. There are also groups of **guerrillas** that want Kashmir to become independent from both countries.

HOT SPOT BRIEFING

WARS IN KASHMIR
India and Pakistan have fought several wars in Kashmir:
- In 1947–1949 the first war was fought
- In 1962, another war happened when Pakistan tried to invade Indian Kashmir
- In 1971 there was another war. After this one, a new border called the Line of Control was agreed.

A Pakistani gun position in the mountains along the border between Indian Kashmir and Pakistani Kashmir.

CIVIL WAR IN PAKISTAN

After independence, the Muslim areas of India became the new country of Pakistan. Pakistan was made up of two separate Muslim areas, West Pakistan which lay to the west of India and East Pakistan which lay to the east of India.

A divided country

The two parts of Pakistan were divided and separated by 1600 kilometres (1000 miles) of Indian territory. Although they were both Muslim areas, their people did not have much else in common. East and West Pakistanis did not even speak the same language.

West Pakistani control

West Pakistan controlled the country's government, trade and armed forces, and held much of the wealth. East Pakistanis became increasingly unhappy about this, and in 1971 **civil war** broke out. East Pakistan declared itself an independent country, Bangladesh.

A bridge in East Pakistan, destroyed during the civil war in 1971.

STATISTICS OF WAR

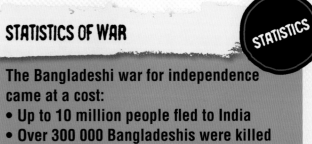

The Bangladeshi war for independence came at a cost:
- Up to 10 million people fled to India
- Over 300 000 Bangladeshis were killed
- 90 000 Pakistani soldiers were taken prisoner.

India joins the conflict

India saw the chance to strike a blow against West Pakistan, which it was still arguing with over Kashmir. India joined the fighting against the West Pakistani forces, which were forced to surrender in December 1971.

Bangladesh today

Today Bangladesh is one of the world's poorest countries. Many people feel that **corrupt** rulers have been one cause of this. Natural disasters, especially floods, have also affected Bangladesh badly. Military leaders have often ruled the country, so people are unable to choose the government that they would like.

'The [Pakistani] Army was confronted with an impossible situation – mass popular uprising within [East Pakistan] and an invasion from without by India ...'

Army officer Pervez Musharraf describing the civil war of 1971. Musharraf later became military ruler of Pakistan.

A Bangladeshi couple wade through floodwaters in June 2007. Large areas of Bangladesh are low-lying, and storms are able to push sea water far inland. This ruins crops and soil.

PAKISTAN AFTER 1971

After 1971, Pakistan controlled only the territory that had previously been known as West Pakistan. This area has its own conflicts, which are often caused by divisions in Pakistani society.

Balochistan

In Balochistan Province, near Pakistan's western border, there was a rebellion against the government during the 1970s, and again after 1999. Some tribal leaders there wanted to separate from Pakistan and have more control of their own affairs. The Pakistan army killed the leader of the rebellion in 2006.

Tribal areas

In northwest Pakistan there are several tribal areas. The people in these areas are different from the rest of Pakistan, and often resist government control. Some tribal leaders have set up alternative governments, run according to Islamic law. Some of these leaders even support the Taliban, a radical Muslim organisation that says society should be run according to harsh Islamic laws.

Army trucks on the streets of Lahore, Pakistan.

HOT SPOT BRIEFING

THE ARMY AND POLITICS
The army is very powerful in Pakistan, and army generals have seized power in 1958–1971 and 1977–1988. In 1999, the army took power once again, led by General Pervez Musharraf.

Outside influences

Pakistan's conflicts have sometimes been made worse by interference from outside the country.

The Taliban from the neighbouring country of Afghanistan supports **Islamic terrorism**. As a result, the USA has urged the Pakistani government to crack down on Taliban supporters. The crackdown has made the Pakistani government unpopular with many of its people, who now see the USA as an enemy of Islam.

The funeral of Benazhir Bhutto.

CONFLICT IN NEPAL

Nepal is a country on India's northern border. For most of its history a single ruler has controlled the whole country. In recent years, this style of government has caused Nepal to become a place of conflict.

1951 revolution

Between 1846 and 1951, Nepal had been ruled by a family called the Ranas. The Ranas used violence to control Nepal. In 1951, a revolution overthrew the Ranas. The revolution gave power back to the royal family. All Nepalis knew and respected the King. The revolutionaries hoped that he could unite their divided country, from the mountains in the north to the lowlands in the south.

Royal rule

Royal rule has not always worked out well for Nepal. The King is supposed to share power with an **elected assembly**, but in recent years he has dismissed the assembly and ruled alone. Many Nepalis have become increasingly unhappy with this.

HOT SPOT BRIEFING

MASSACRE AT THE PALACE
In 2001, Prince Dipendra, a senior member of Nepal's royal family, went on a violent rampage through the royal palace. He killed the King, Queen and seven other members of the royal family, and then shot himself.

Pro-democracy protesters on the streets of Kathmandu, Nepal's capital city, in 2006.

Demands for democracy

Most Nepalis would like more democracy in their country. In 1971 and 1990, there were violent demonstrations, with protesters demanding that the King give up some of his power. In addition, in 1996 communist rebels began a fight against Nepal's current rulers.

Change in Nepal

In 2007, democrats and rebels joined together to strip away the King's powers. They struggled to agree on a new constitution for Nepal, however, and it seemed uncertain whether their alliance could last.

'This has given a message to the international community and terrorists all over the world that no conflict can be resolved by guns. It can be done by dialogue.'

Nepali Prime Minister Girija Prasad Koirala in 2006. He had just signed a peace deal, ending an armed conflict that had been going on for ten years.

Rebel troops in Nepal. Until the peace deal of 2006, rebel forces controlled large areas of the countryside and regularly launched attacks on the Nepali army.

CONFLICT IN SRI LANKA

Sri Lanka is an island country off the southern tip of India. It is home to two main peoples, the Sinhalese and the Tamils. Disagreements between the two peoples have made Sri Lanka a place of violent conflicts.

People

Sri Lanka's peoples are very different from one another:

- Sinhalese people make up about 75 per cent of Sri Lanka's people. They speak Sinhala, and are mainly **Buddhists**.
- Tamil people make up about 20 per cent of the population. They speak Tamil, and are mostly Hindus.

Sinhalese domination

Sinhalese people dominate Sri Lanka's politics, trade and government. During the 1970s and 1980s, Tamil people began to feel that they were suffering as a result of the Sinhalese domination. They began to demand a separate land of their own in northeastern Sri Lanka.

'Tamil children feel there is no hope for their lives. They all want to go abroad, because there is nothing for them here.'

A Hindu leader during the 1990s, explaining the situation for young Tamils.

The aftermath of a suicide bomb attack in Sri Lanka.

The Tamil Tigers

Some Tamil groups decided to fight to get their own country. The most notorious group is the Tamil Tigers. In 1983 the Tigers attacked government troops in Tamil areas. Thousands of people died, and many Tamils fled to India. Ever since, the Tigers and the government have been fighting, although sometimes they agree on a temporary ceasefire.

In 2002 the Tigers stopped demanding a separate Tamil country, but they and the government still find it difficult to agree exactly how to live together peacefully.

HOT SPOT BRIEFING

SUICIDE BOMBING
The Tamil Tigers were one of the first terrorist groups to use suicide bombing. A suicide bombing is when the bomber sets off a bomb strapped to his or her own body, killing themselves and people nearby.

Armed Tamil Tigers controlling a roadblock in northeast Sri Lanka.

PROSPECTS FOR THE FUTURE

The Indian subcontinent's different peoples and religions have always found it hard to live together peacefully. Today, though, there seem to be signs that in some places this is changing.

India

India still has a bitter dispute with Pakistan over Kashmir. However, today many Indians are more focused on the benefits of their fast-growing **economy** than arguments with their neighbours. India's new wealth can provide its people with higher wages, good accommodation, new clothes and other goods.

Pakistan

Pakistan has two major challenges ahead. First, there is a conflict between the military government and those who want democracy to return to Pakistan. Second, there is conflict between those who want a Muslim government and those who do not. Both of these problems will have to be solved if Pakistan is to be at peace.

Election violence in Bangladesh in 2006. Elections in the Indian subcontinent often suffer from violence, as the supporters of different parties try to prevent each other from voting.

NUCLEAR WEAPONS
Both India and Pakistan have the ability to make nuclear bombs. If used, these weapons are capable of wiping out the whole population of both countries. This means that any future armed conflict between them could have much more serious effects than in the past.

Nepal

In 2007, the communists and democrats in Nepal started to plan for elections, so that a government chosen by all Nepal's people could run the country, instead of the King.

Sri Lanka

In 2008, the Sri Lankan Government said that its latest ceasefire agreement with the Tamil Tigers was over. Government forces restarted their campaign to defeat the Tigers, who quickly responded with a new wave of suicide bomb attacks.

Bangladesh

Bangladesh's biggest problem is **poverty**. Bangladeshis are among the poorest people in the world, although its rulers are usually wealthy. Spreading the wealth more evenly would improve the lives of ordinary people.

'I don't think that anyone seriously fears that the world can be blown to pieces altogether. But what one can fear and rightly so are regional things, like in ... India [and] Pakistan ...'

Hans Blix, former UN weapons inspector, in 2007 on his fears of possible nuclear conflict.

A Pakistani missile is tested. Missiles like this can carry nuclear weapons over 2000 kilometres (1250 miles).

FACTFINDER

INDIA

The flag of India

Capital New Delhi

Area 3 287 600 square kilometres
(1 269 300 square miles)

Population 1 129 866 154

Rate of population change +1.6% per year

Life expectancy 68.6 years

Religions Hindu 81%

Muslim 13%

Christian 2%

Sikh 2%

Other 2%

Main exports Petroleum products, textile
goods, gems and jewellery, engineering goods,
chemicals, leather goods

Gross Domestic Product per person* US$2700

PAKISTAN

The flag of Pakistan

Capital Islamabad

Area 803 940 square kilometres
(310 400 square miles)

Population 164 741 924

Rate of population change +1.8% per year

Life expectancy 63.8 years

Religions Muslim 97%

(Sunni 77%)

(Shi'ite 20%)

Other 3%

Main exports Textiles, rice, leather goods, sports
goods, chemicals, carpets and rugs

Gross Domestic Product per person* US$2600

NEPAL

The flag of Nepal

Capital Kathmandu

Area 147 180 square kilometres
(56 825 square miles)

Population 28 901 790

Rate of population change +2.1% per year

Life expectancy 60.6 years

Religions Hindu 81%

Buddhist 11%

Muslim 4%

Other 4%

Main exports Carpets, clothing, leather goods,
jute goods, grain

Gross Domestic Product per person* US$1100

SRI LANKA

The flag of Sri Lanka

Capital Colombo (commercial),
Sri Jayawardenapura-Kotte (administrative)

Area 65 610 square kilometres
(25 330 square miles)

Population 20 926 315

Rate of population change +1.0% per year

Life expectancy 74.8 years

Religions Buddhist 69%

Muslim 8%

Hindu 7%

Christian 6%

Other 10%

Main exports Textiles, clothing, tea and spices,
diamonds and other gems, coconut products,
rubber goods, fish

Gross Domestic Product per person* US$4100

* Gross Domestic Product, or GDP, per person is the total value of all the goods and services produced by a country in a year divided by the number of people in the country. (Source for statistics: *CIA World Factbook*)

GLOSSARY

architecture style and technique of building

Aryan invaders people from central Asia who took control of northern India from about 1500 CE onwards

Aung San Suu Kyi leader of the National League for Democracy in Myanmar (Burma), a group trying to win control of the country back from its military rulers

Buddhists followers of the Buddhist religion

ceasefire temporary end to fighting

Civil Rights movement campaign for African-Americans to have the same rights as other US citizens

civil war war between different groups in the same country

corrupt dishonest, willing to accept a payment of money in return for giving someone unfair help

culture things that make a group of people distinctive, such as their language, clothes, food, music, songs and stories

democracy system where every qualified person in a country is able to vote to decide how the country should be governed

economy all the activities that make money, for example making or growing goods and selling them

elected assembly group of people chosen by the people of a country or region to help govern it

equal rights all people having the same rights as others, whatever the colour of their skin

founded begun

guerrillas fighters who use hit-and-run tactics to attacks their enemies

independence ability to act alone, without control from someone or something else

Islamic terrorism terrorism by extreme members of the Muslim religion, using illegal violence against those who they see as their enemies

Mughal Empire empire that ruled large areas of India between 1526 and the mid-1800s

Partition Division of British India into India and Pakistan in 1947

poverty lack of enough money to pay for food and shelter

rebels people fighting against the government

subjects people ruled by a king, queen or other government

taxes payments demanded by the government

terrorist person or people using violence to scare others

United Nations organisation set up after World War II that aims to help countries end disputes without fighting

INDEX

LLOYD GEORGE SCHOOL,
830 PINE STREET,
KAMLOOPS, B. C.
V2C 3A1

LLOYD GEORGE SCHOOL,
830 PINE STREET,
KAMLOOPS, B. C.
V2C 3A1